ROBERT P. ARTHUR:
Selected Works

Robert Arthur

NORTHAMPTON HOUSE PRESS

Cover photo by Chris Glennon.
Cover design by Northampton House Press.
Northampton House Press trade paper edition, 2019, ISBN 978-1-937997-98-4.
Library of Congress Control Number: 2019939512.

9 8 7 6 5 4 3 2

SELECTED WORKS

Contents

The Arrow

From the bow of the bent branch
    the arrow split my chest

Yes, I will ride a white stallion, its
    arc of neck and seat of bone

As black blood poured from my open
    mouth, a shoulder slumped and slid from
    my chest   Then the other

While my eyes stared wide from a central
    shaft that toppled down into night-
    shadowed grass

I could see the stars beating, the many
    hearts of heaven, and then the stallion
    came racing down an avenue of moon

I could hear the spigots, the many spigots
    turning on in the lost forest of my love, their
    waters rushing

The cold descending to where my love
    was sleeping with her foxes

Yes, I would have her arms around me,
    the softness of flesh, the hardness of bone

Yes, I was weary, the houses were sinking
    into the earth, their lifted skirts covered
    with mud

I remembered the horses and the names
    of horses, and heard someone calling

1

out the names of horses

Persephone, I cried, and pulled myself up

By a fist in the petals of her shining black hair
    in the forest of myrtle

In the deepening woods   in the deepening woods
    in its habit of darkness

And now
    sang the crocus, yes now the crocus sang
    with the sun gone out, in its habit of darkness

On the Death of Darlin' Ann
(To Sunday Abbott)

When the full moon pales at high niche
I walk the Celtic way, so find my love a-dreaming
In realms above the bay. I hear the nightjars
Scraping, above the ocean's roar, and feel
The tides a-turning like the opening of a door

Somewhere waves are breaching
The shingle of the strand. The wind is high
As heaven and silver fish take wing
To sing the songs of nightingales- Oh,
To sing the songs they sing

Somewhere the storm is waning
But here it rages on. My cottage lights are trembling
By fields of aching corn. But kerchiefs still are streaming
Beyond the western key
Before the sea shall find me, I shall find the sea

Shadows fall into the eyes
Of animals: motile underbranches
Of night, having breath.
Pensive umbrae flow into vines
Of bramble fruit-- blackberry, raspberry,
Olallieberry-- ingesting light,
Mum as Pluto. Winter nights
Roll unbroken by intervening day.
The painting whispers dusk.
A colonial child in a Roman toga
Ascends into a carriage rocked
By oscillating dark and the hoot
Of an owl in a distant tree.
The symbolism's clear.
A black horse stands by a pasture stone.
The boy is dead. There is no heir.

Breakthrough.doc

On a night when

Words

flowed

And seemed

liquid on a page

And all ran together like strange
Varieties of eels following each other

Over rocks and peeking into hollows
Of dark shadow and clumped somethings clumping

Each sensing the other

Growing pregnant with the other
And birthing with each other and many anythings

Running off into many realms   and birthing

Perhaps, Yes, birthing

Perhaps
Birthing with each other

and adopting young everythings modifying one another and
extending the other to somehow run together and then to run on

Into somethings diminishing and swelling up with each other
guessing

About one another and always and only referring to each other to make multiple everythings collapsing into each other with connectives like elastic bringing them back together forming loving spoons

Fitting each other and clattering without space

Transferring elements of one another to each of the other and so bringing forth bowls of some liquid or another with which they anoint one another, bringing forth color that swarms over the page with every shade and hue of prismatic color and someone turns a wheel that makes everything white and causes a general jubilation that makes everything want to go home in general and so everything goes back home, finally. Everything goes back, goes back into color

where everything dances with the others, first springing into color and then not, then yes, growing back into trees I had missed

and sky I had missed, and earth I had missed, and sea I had missed that was dancing under boats I had missed dancing on sea under sky I had missed over earth I had missed and then everything I had missed was going back as if drawn by shape, drawing forth image filled with stars growing together going back through ages

of clumps in hollows through the eyes of eels in water to words again to a second jubilation and took on the appearance of a golden ball

and then I was happy because a poem appeared

a poem whose every word was filled with whole libraries of dancing books come together and the whole thing was perfect, drawn into place by a force of symmetry and grace and was perfect, the whole thing, perfect

with shadows balancing with good into a moral sense and every word and word within word explaining the whole thing and one another in regard to place and was perfect, and all things of the senses of everything were joining and touching and dividing and extending and feeling and explaining everything to everything else

It was perfect

I was exultant. I was exultant and clapping my hands and streaming with tears and everything was breathing, drawing away and going back in together to live through the ages and I could detach and let it go on through the ages without me. I could detach. No. I loved it. I loved it. I could not detach.

I heard a voice in my empty room, behind me

Dad   dad   daa…ad

Sort of musical like that, but not
Maybe plaintive, but no, not that

With a tone…with a tone that asked a question, but not quite
With a tone finding something, but no, not quite

With a tone that was like…
With a tone that was exactly like…

Yes, exactly like that
With a tone in still air   in air   that was exactly like…

The tone of someone who couldn't find something with his eyes
That his heart knew was there

The Centaur
(For Richard Williams)

Beauty in buckle and a muddy track
In the grip of an oval that always comes back
The horseman canters by in bones that creak
The chickens are waking, yawning in Greek

Achilles Achilles cluck
Achilles Achilles cluck

Ariat boot, hoof, extension and glide
A horse walks by with a man inside
Pirouette, piaffe, passage, half pass
Cock-a-doodle-do, halt, and release

Puck, puck, puck, puck, pawk
Puck, puck, puck, puck, pawk

The circling hawks end their talks
Praise Gods for luck and hades below
Stirrup and bit chorus in squawks
The arrow's straight and sure the bow
Troy is falling, Troy is falling
Levade, courbette, ballotade, capriole

The reins fall gently as Olympian snow
The horse thinks it's going where it wants to go
Then a Flying Change by the trembling gate
Snatches a clap from the lowing sky

Centaurus Kentauroi

Darkness (deposes)

A tidal bore,
A hiding place
A torrent of black in a color space

Water breaks
To a sound of weeping and the "gnashing of teeth"

The ice-cold ice

Ineluctable, stable
Beyond the light
Of Dante's circle

Deorc, Sceadu

Jaws of darkness
Swallow skimmers of love
In the moon's stone face

An absence of light
In the slumping of soldiers

A demented woman calls
To the ghost of her lover
She has found in a mirror

Who's to say that life is not horrible
In contrast with brightness?

(Achromatic)

In the case
Of darkness, black as black

As a void of grackle

Invisible light
In sable

Begins, ends, extends
Secret, and evil

A blackamoor stands at a slave ship's anvil

Cattle Sleeping or Sleeping Cattle
(For Leonardo of Pisa, AKA Fibonacci (1170-1250), whose
mathematical sequence suggests that numerous natural forms
replicate the shape of the heavens)

Dusting snow finds scraps
Of cattle posing in hoarfrost
And not yet lost. Through
Quiet dark, vestigial bone
And horn and hide hurl
Bells that peal down paths
Of oblivion's clatter

And we are dying in the
Cheat-grass turnings of the wheel
And engines of threshing.
Cold fires have laid the cattle out
On trays of leaves for burning.
Cattle turn dun, flashing hooves
Devolving, melting into flame

Cattle sleeping, sleeping cattle
Thy horn's slow curve extends
The shadow of the Herder's crook
Through the night's pavilion.
O blessed stem of the Milky Way
Lowing of whorls
In the gyre of morning

In winter's flower, I shall go cenotaph singing

Aunt Ursula Birdwood, she had an old sow
And it died in her own park-o

The Turning

She unclasps her necklace
And turns toward a window, singing
With rain, and in the music of her
Singing there is a fluidity of
Phrase and return to the prelude
Of her turning-

    and the clasp of the
Rose of Sharon's chain is again
Undone and softly pulled past her
Upturned nose and through
Kumbuck black hair to a cracked
White table of marble snow-

    and again
The Murano glass of the Rose
Of Sharon is dropped to the
Table of fallen light by fingers
That move beyond her lips
In the turning-

    and pomegranate
Tips of her breasts lyrically
Uplift to the infant tongue
Of the rainy day, and
She in her flesh is all nutmeg,
Ginger and smoke-

    in the bouquet
Of her body, in her dark
Kissed eyes and luxury of hair that
In the gyre of her shoulders
Drops to her fundamental
Bifurcated self, perfumed with-

    powders of rain

And sweet in its shadows, sighing
Thin legs moving to the window
Her waist revolving, her elbows
And arms simultaneously following,
To the freshness of a garden-

    breeze, flowing
And she swings, translucent
In lilac, before the crosses
Of the window with legs spread
Wide and the beads in her body
To be blown into children-

And I am with her in the pink leaves
Of her upturned earth and petals of dark
In the yawing concert of straight
Shoulders and angular limbs,
In the bladed architecture of her
Body. Oh shield and sword

    Oh harbor and sail

And me an old man, remembering
In a broken bed, eyes shut with weeping,
gasp following gasp in convulsions of
longing, for she who once turned before
me in a window of rain

Singing now with a voice too much like love

Song of the Theologians

Yahweh

The mountain god
Was first a god of storm
And then of war

The Lord is a man of war

And we had a covenant with him
We people of the blood
And sling and blade

But if you...do all that I say,
Then I will be an enemy to your enemies,
And an adversary to your adversaries

All war was religious war
And the land of Canaan was a sacred land

We people of the blood
Sought oracular counsel
Through dreams

Through the Urim
Or the chief Priest Ephod
Or prophets
Or the witch of Endor

Then sanctified ourselves
With cleansing rituals
And abstinence from sexual intercourse

Our camps were swept free
Of human refuse
We camped on sacred ground

And the Lord fought with us
As banner, shield, and sword
When the cry went up
And spread from man to man
And slave to boy
The trumpet blared

And all were hosts
And our Lord the Lord of hosts
And his anointed generals, judges

The spirit of God came upon the judges

But still we trembled

And there in the sunlight
That disappeared in the shadows
Of night

Or in the starlight
That receded into the light of day

We grew idolatrous, covenant or none

We listened for foxes
In the wilderness
And the nine hundred chariots of iron
Of Sisera

That ravaged our vineyards
And left our children slain

And so Deborath a prophetess and judge
Of the tribe of Ephraim

Arose in a woman's clay

And so we took the dead into our houses
And persons of the family and mourners and slaves
And all lamented in lamplight and the lamplight's shadow
Lamented with moaning and the smiting of breasts
And ejaculations of grief, calling out for the Lord

And so Deborah said to us
If a father is dead, the oldest son will bestow
The last tokens

So Deborah said

So Joseph, in his grief, closed the eyes of Jacob
And the circles of mourners extended to housetops and streets
And someone was first to rend his garments
And with coarse sackcloth to wrap his waist

So Deborah said

And someone laid aside the ornaments of the living
To sit in ash without shoes, to draw blood with knives
From his own flesh, to cry out for Israel
To shave or tonsure, to throw dust on his head

And that person was followed, Deborah said

Then everyone listened

Though Deborah was but the wife of the unknown Lapidoth
She was the keeper of the tabernacle lamps
As befit a woman who would be mother of Israel

She lived in a small house on the road
Between Ramah and Beth-el
In the hill country of Ephraim

And in the furnace of day and cold of night
Sat amid the olive trees

Under the royal date tree
And gave advice and prophecy

And so Deborah said

Absence is silence in this death land
For silence is what is meant by death here
For in death there is no talk in the quiet moon
Unless there is wind, and wind is not talk

As you learn on the desert. Nor is wind movement
It is absence, itself, as silence is absence
So when I walked into the dead land
To find the Lord, I walked into the absence
Of all things, into the absence of myself
Not just into the desert, as I knew it
But into a silence, from which we will bring the Lord

Foxfire

Sunlight soaked into damp logs and stumps
Where mushrooms grow
Like souls unearthed
Slips out as foxfire, cold fire, mountain light
Glowing faintly green,
An elfin trace carnivaling
In the glim
Of rich earth and bark sodden as dung

It gives off glum light, absorbed
For decades, now released by oxygen,
Fungi, and the crush of rot.
In darkest night

Maybe even haints find
Emeralds in the creek's undercut
Or city lights in pulled up stumps,
Or splotches of fire
Creeping up roots from the dank
To sprawl like moonlight on moldering leaves
Or fly like eerie fire with wings.
Some say

Jesus throws foxfire into waterfalls
And watches it tumble over rocks
Shedding eyes of lime
In wild hydraulics of winding dark
Bound to be broken, again and again

In pain   to shine.

Now the Hour of Advent Drawing Nigh
(For Albert Einstein)

Now the hour of Advent drawing nigh
Drops kits to skulks in amber cold
School bells ring in winter's flower
Comes the hanging of the green
Where wreaths beset the heavy hill
And snow shall comfort fallen stone

For snow shall comfort fallen stone
And death shall blaze in brazen tombs
For this is my beloved, my …
Holy Physicist, in Apocalypse
For whom in dreaming sight
Time's flush of sun and moon are one

And now the hour of Advent calls forth
The fire-eyed grain. Wretched earth
From killing frost shall heave its young
Herald foxes bark as seamless
Light shall bend, and dimensions begin
Their headlong rush into eternity

All salads here are served
With onions, tomatoes, grief
And green peppers; fat-free
Ranch, blue cheese, French
Or peppercorn Parmesan.
She has ashes in her hair
And weeps at the mention
Of Harlan, Kentucky.
She says she's a brakeman's
Daughter pried loose
From his upside down,
Belly-ripped hanging.
All men got brains of coal,
She says, thinking of trains,
Unbuttoning her blouse,
And swatting my hand.
Kin I see you naked, I say.
She's listening close to
The veins of blood in my
Bumble of words. A
Beehive opens in her
Abdomen, succulent, sweet
And golden. She's
Delicious on my fingers.
Honey runs from my mouth.
There is blood in the comb of
The angel of darkness,
The taste of humming
Where the lion sits down
With the lamb

Seawater winters in oblique light
washed by rain
Terns skim the marsh waters
Ice scrapes the rushes
clean, the tumps, asleep,
slipping into shadow
Soon, white fire behind the pin-holed
        skein of dark will be stars
 Shadows fall into my brain
        like depakote and loxapine

I was not comprehensible, but there was a nurse to wash me.

The cottages with their curtains
        have dreams of breathing
All night long there will be a prowling of dragon-
        flies, in skulks,
        heads dropping into moons
I am thinking of a darkened road, my best feet
        skittering, the black skimmers
        of evening gone to roost
        with gulls
        in the shallows

A woman is weeping but she is not my woman.

The boy on the table has bled out internally, a gash on
        his head, bones speaking their language,
        a rooting syringe
        drawing blood from his heart
His brains have been knocked from one side
Of his head to the other
He had a father and mother
In Hazleton, Pennsylvania

Pale Moon Let Hang Thy Ropes of Haunted Hair

Pale moon let hang thy ropes of haunted hair
Black trees may lift their skirts of root, insane
The dying leaves curl like hands in prayer

The killing frost may blow and evil bear
Or stars may crisp to prove the plowman's bane
Pale moon let hang thy ropes of haunted hair

Shelved ice may calve but who exults and where?
Wolf pups may howl like ghosts in silvered rain
The dying leaves curl their hands in prayer

The child may die and yet his eyeteeth bare,
Cold dumb, in snow, beneath the thicket's shame
Pale moon let hang thy ropes of haunted hair

Death feeds on life and finds it fleeting near
In shot bush, or whistle of a distant train
The dying leaves curl their hands in prayer

Winter drops its lid of marbled air
The harvest owl may swoop and call thy name
Pale moon let hang thy ropes of haunted hair
The dying leaves curl like hands in prayer

Starry Night

VAN GOGH'S VOICE

There's a terrible loneliness in the open air of day
I've grown to prefer the night of Saint-Rémi

A woman in the distance cries

Starry starry night

In the starlight   in the light reflected   in dark water
I once found two lovers…
… strolling the length of a boulevard
     under the dark brocade of night

A child is born in Bethlehem

Starry starry night

And a woman cries

for the Savior who comes is a Christ who comes in flesh
     not paint or clay

too real for her
     and for all the world   too real

And I recall all this, all the turbulence of his birth…and
consequence
In this Starry night of Saint-Rémi
     there's something written…
     something heavily dark with light
     …and more congenial than all the prayers
     of day

No more images of God, for me, will do

Only this Starry night will do...

...circumlocutions of the spheres...
the rising temper of celestial sea, mystic union
    and release

I eschew theology

And a woman cries beyond the pavilion

Starry starry night

night of night forms... dynamic sprawl...

In the night sky, riding

In the night sky
there's an anomalous complex of moon and sun and earth shadow
locked in surprise
...in eclipse...
all reminiscent of that woman of the apocalypse....
Oh, you remember her...
girded with the sun and moon and crowned by stars

...in part a recollection of stars from a night sky long ago in Arles

We fools for God are hardly above
hallucinating everything
hallucinating love

Everyone is mad enough in the modern world
I do not invent pictures of God

I extend myself, as stars extend themselves... in continuous swirls

Starry starry night

On such a night I paint the stars, in fever
and find a newborn child
curled in fire, waking
at night in the dragon's belly
of Revelations

Memories of glory drift, confused

Turning from nature, I find in the mind's eyes
these two gigantic, spiral nebulae
entwined
...these aureoles of sky... an unreal moon... the Milky Way in a
broad band of light

A cypress flame, formed
in shadow,
breaking the arc of a cosmic coupling

and a woman cries in the night's pavilion

The loneliness of the town
echoes
the aspirations of a steeple
transcending
the earth's horizon

as I have done...in my ragged coat
and outworn pain

Every object and region has its own rhythm

There's a cold blustering of wind...
so many stars and possibilities
for whom the retiring woman is--

Heaven reels in contrast with the earth below

God is a lighthouse in eclipse-says Hugo

Symmetrical rectangles of light…of town…
lie submerged by entanglements of sky
    in an impulsive, sweeping flood
of strokes… and the orange moon
hangs, incredibly, over all

with a light between its horns

A woman cries beyond the dark pavilion

Starry starry night

Starry starry night of Saint-Rémi

VAN GOGH'S VOICE

In the dark, blue-green
and brown colors of the earth
in the cellar shadows
held aloft by the bulbous light

in their potato modeling
and potato skins
in wrinkled knuckling
they eat potatoes, clumsily

under the single lamp
from a common platter
Each one who has labored
eats potatoes, speaking

wordlessly, of having beaten back
solitude and the weather
Each in the shadows of his own corner
of the communal table

stares within to the edge
of loneliness and hunger
It is so much more to paint the eyes of people
than to paint cathedrals

Legacy

Darkness falls through winter's
end to spring-rises up stems
from earth to flowers, and through
the gaping blossom spurts

as shadow. Grandfather
tells the cooing child—"All the bright,
heliotropic towers of the garden
are but gurgling fountains of the dark."

"Hush," he whispers. "Honeybees
swarm from the rose's tip
with sweet dark crushed
into explosive air—and you'll swim

half blind, the wretched deluge
of the corruption's spray. And may never know it
for what it is—darkness, darkness
Darkness is its name."

Essay on Painters

(Painter: Appalachian for panther or mountain lion)

Painters
on the trail at night
rumbling deep in the chest
their footfalls light

pat, pat, pat, pat

stopping when you do

I don't believe
Painters are
Formed of rain

Some people do

Painters
circle round, and
double back

scream from ledges
like a woman cut

Babies et,
have been covered by leaves
like scat

Painters got
the broad paws
and hair between its toes

pat   pat   pat

You hear a thump
of a tail in your path

pitch black

painters
flowing through rock
like coal

Ain't never seen
one

'cept in ghost form
the brain builds
when you look
at tracks

You'd be struck
by how
damp

and shallow they are

pat   pat   pat

toe pads like raindrops
on the dusty road

The painter's running
tail arching
high

rounding bait piles
in snow
to where I'm
waiting

My arms spread out and extended by branches
and
I'm screaming out

"Painter, git! Git on outta here!"

as my tongue first learned
ten thousand years ago

Appearances

I have taken a ruler to the moon
When full moons replicate overhead
As timeless fruit

I am suffering a moon delusion

Paradigms flow in neurological ether
Ethics float loose wired in the brain

In the moon of Gandhi   in Gandhi's moon
A single psychopath with a knife may exterminate a city

I have taken a ruler to the moon
When crescent moons seem bitten like wafers
And dripping over the horizon

Violence appears to be ethical

Just as the moons' blood fills a bucket of rock
Just as a wolf drops young mice to the teeth of its young

I have taken a ruler to the ruler of the moon

*It wasn't enough that the Sermon on the Mount was a confession of
his heart
He had to be the son of man, the son of God
The child of the virgin bride*

Flung into the ephemeral

I have taken a ruler to the moon
And found its mute-winged locus arching
Over the moist earth of my squat, earthen house

In wisps of shadow   in wisps of wisps of shadow

I have taken a ruler to the ruler of the ruler of the moon

Spruce

Something slightly dark and old lives here
After the autumnal equinox

In lichen weather

Rainwater puddles in beads on the black
Blown feather

Melting into shadow

Raven curses hang as misty sheets of wash
Over long, shadowed poles.
The jack pine skitters

Tatters of paper birch rattle in the breeze
Like the parchment of ancient scrolls

Needles punctuate the dark

Flakes fall, white as tufts of fur

Mushroom puffs grown deadly red
Bloom in stools and tables of ancient furniture

This is the deep black spruce forest
Of ankle-deep moss in evening shade
The white wolf, Skoll
Chases the sun to the western sky

Something runs here below the whispered river

This is the boreal forest of foxglove
And grouse, the maple leaf floating
On the hushed dark face of the solstice pond

Hati, the dark one, devours the moon

No ghost or tales here of the fruited vine
Or singular sparrow

On the pond ice the powdered snow
Reiterates the swirl of wind
The thickened brush pants of death

Paw prints stretch the desolate ice sheeted lake
In ironic signature to the howled banged drum

of concussive doom

Without the wolf there would be no time

Last Rites

Because words were not enough he left
    No note
Only a last line dropped in air, and
    Below the bridge
His bones, illegible
Scrawled on an ice sheet of the Potomac river

His muse, from her reluctant bed
    Gaped and grinned
Recalled his horny iambics, his
    Fumbling meter

(Not even the water would take him in)

Sunday Seizure

I took her down as my father taught me
Not waiting for others

As the benediction ended

My arms locked around hers
The organ stopped and someone swooned
Blood flew from her tongue
For lack of a spoon   for lack of a spoon

I took her down as her heels danced me round

Her body on top of mine
Upsetting the vestibule candles

Hubbub   hubbub
Her lips blubbery with blood

My own blood
Streaming from my hare-shotten lip

And somebody waving one of those paper Jesus fans

I held on for the Lord, head banging the floor
De dum   De dum

Until her thrashing was over

She had the Devil inside her, someone shrieked
Now   He's   in her son

Being born   being born
Busy being born

Later, I entered her hospital room
Her tongue was painted the color plum

1950, Cape Charles, Virginia

The night my mother left
my father drank and cried
holding his glass to hide his mouth

Next day we went out for shark
my brother and I held on for pride
and jerked our lines

from the undertow. We caught dog shark
Bill's to port, mine to the right
and my father took them by their throats

Because he'd forgotten the butcher knife
(and sharks are dangerous in rocking boats)
He stood upright and didn't curse us
for pulling them in

But cursed the man and the morning
light that made him span
a boat of children
with a snapping shark in either hand

Why couldn't he have been God?

He squeezed Bill's shark until its
guts came busting out
Then smacked my shark against the
boat to break its back

Why couldn't he have been God?
I'd give the job to anyone
who could handle sharks like that

Murdered girl, curled, in frost
Naked to the rumpled air
Moonlight slips through expiring leaves
Finding strings of shadow
Never have you lain alone
In your grove of shot bush

Speckled alder

Shadows plunge in excitation
To the primal gut, racketing
Leaves from Trees of Heaven.
Never has there been
Tribal hurt not plucked
By brokered man

In raving blood

Worms oscillate, descend
And eat the shadows' curse
To drill time's crust.
Church bells chime their
Random notes. Dimensions
Unearth and Black Elders, shaken
Drop flowered

Rain

Light bends around your weight
And all things declare their eternal fall
Through shelves of space
…to where you are

We are all murdered: all

The Forest

Nibbled leaves
in carpets of ginseng
weed, where
the roots hold
deep t' the
forest floor
's a sure sign
of deer browsing
for centuries
hooking horns
with honey trees

Haints and
polecats sleep
troubled sleep
here, by Ball Creek
the night ripe
with deer
hooves sharp as
spades digging in
the holler dark
where the wild ginseng
blows

Family men
speaking of bringing in
Cherokee crystals
and pearly river
stones.
Funny way
folks fear
when the ghost
deer come
and babies quick born
drop
blue as plums

You'll hear women singing
in cabins by th' road

*Modern medicine has determined that the Blue People of
Appalachia were afflicted by a rare blood disorder called
"methemoglobinemia."*

17
(From Hymn to the Chesapeake)

I have come to the place where the clocks wind down
and the end begins
with the ticking of new life in the wild sea grasses
I have come from the hollow places of Eastern Shore towns
Silver Beach and Painter
from the fairgrounds at Keller, where even from the hollows
mothers trot out their children
their jams and glasses

Oh, father light, in the passing
in the new movement of water in the winds' releasing
in the dying leaves,   which have in love knots

in the dark boughs and branches left shadows of their forms
their colors their functions

I have come to the grove of wounded trees
You, in soft silk, walking beside me

Where night from its encampment in air
Comes on with its whistles and cannons
And the quiet murdered animals move enfilade
To a misty desecration as unilateral as cold
in the islands

And it is all because of your soft hand's easing
that the bud yard shines

And the whole sodden landscape sobs suddenly
with glory

Snakes

Went Hensley bit 446 times died of the 447th at the age of 75

Died of belching blood and writhing
on the floor   beloved   by the Lord

I can't understand why people can't see it
Right there it is in the Bible for the man that believes

Study the Lord's saying. That's not my saying

...they shall take up serpents... Writ right there

Copperheads bite you quicker
but the rattlesnake busts your heart

Know'd a woman put the rattler in her bosom
Let the copperheads climb the rope of her hair

Faith's healing water... pours...from the word

Used to bring the snakes in a flat box
in the front of the church, slide 'em under the low bench

behind the altar, hissing, till the speakin' was through

ié ieus éó ou éó óua! iiii éééé uuuu óóóó aaaaa, éi

and the choir sang, Moses, Pull Off Your Shoes

Pastor says, *Take the serpents up...*

Pit viper's got that triangular head
pits dug deep for lidless eyes

If y' kiss its throat it will get riled up and go insane

Imagine the eyes blushed red and the devil's tail

stiff in yer grip

I been bit twelve times cause my faith give out

Now the Bible calls those who preach
different, *grievous wolves*

Grievous wolves,

Bible says, *shall come among you, not sparing the flock*

It was revealed to me in the Bible where it said, *Take ' em up*

One Sunday a man brought one, said, *Can I bring it in?*
and someone said, *Yeah, bring it in*

and the man said, the preacher got to say, *Yes*
and I went out to 'im and hollered, *Bring it in*

I would not have you ignorant or simple, like some
Declare your faith by fire and snake

and poison…

Sunday after…One by one, I said. *Take 'em up*

Pull off you Shoes, Moses. Drums in the sky

I think the most serpents I ever handled at once were nine

Women weeping, praying, waving their arms
snakes in their hands

If you're losing your faith, get shed of it quick
A neighbor one Sunday bit three times

He had a carnal mind

Don't touch no snake if there's been a fuss in the church

I seen twelve men die…I am falling asleep…
Night of fog…women crying…in my dreams

Mountain rears up in a viper's hood

Red rivers run down
like fangs filled with blood

Poison streams into the heavy wood

I ain't never goin' to quit it

Whoop for the Lord
Whoop for the Lord

Copperhead's easy for babies and children
Rattler's holy

Thar's a whole lot here
Folk don't understand

Whitewater on the Potomac

It's a matter of feel.
When the current's strong,
the canoe will turn either way
at the drop of a paddle.

Just lean and adjust the
angle of the blade
like so. How much for sure
the river will teach you,

And if the rocks
come rushing, avoid the urge
to push off with a hand
or a rifle. Instead

Using water as if it were
something to hold you, dip the blade
and pull the canoe toward it
like so—into the channel

That way you'll live
for the rooster tails of another day
It's a matter of feel,
of leaning, of adjusting the angle,

of pulling, not pushing,
of finding the channel,
of dipping in the dark, leaning out,
and bracing with the paddle,

Of believing the water will hold you.
Do not, therefore, love fear
too much, or depth, or the whitening curl.
some keeper will claim you.

And never, into turbulence
take anyone with you
who cannot eddy, in and out
as the manuals say. Rather

Practice each day the river's art.
Slip over ledges with trim
of your own making, not feeling
the paddling. Like so. Begin.

Thunder in Wintertime

Thunder in wintertime
means a weather change

Last night I dreamed

Cherokee trailing over red clay
leaving a blood road in snow

Now will-o'-the-wisps
and wraiths rise from sinkholes

Got a gut full of shot
…this place this life

Bleeding from worm holes
I'm all used up

But of a morning in the hills
beauty comes in a flush of light

Death whispers in the trees and the trees repeat everything

Flakes of snow ride the cold mountain draughts

Blue river runs through emerald wood
forks like a tongue

in shook rocks

It'll seem a formality
When the horseman comes

From Crazy Horse's Woman

Black Shawl: How He Filled Me with Horror

So this is how Pgeon gave me to him in the quiet bower
In the nest of singing birds
With the dew wrapped round me

So this is how the great God Crazy Horse found me in the quiet
light
In the falling light of morning's glow

My face and scalp vermilion
My hair so shining, soft

My dress of white buckskin, teethed so soft
So deep-beaded, yoke blue, so wing-sleeved and fringed with
particles of bone
So blue with powder

And this is how I received him:

Not as free maiden, but as Black Shawl the given
Called Black Buffalo Woman
For my names are legion

As Black Shawl the dew-wrapped
Naked
Crying out for heat   for blood
For stars

For he was a phantom of ice
So snow in the heart and lips and fingers and flower

So glacial

I cried for his soul
In the light-softened bower where the sky hung naked

And the dew had gathered

So many dead men lay weeping inside him

I loved him, loved him
As my mother instructed

Still, Oh Mother, I cried, Oh Slow Bear, my mother
He is frigid in the flower
So North and Wind and Hell
All coming inside me
So filling me with truth
With death
With horror!

From Crazy Horse's Woman

Black Shawl: How He Let Me Go

So Crazy Horse took me into his lodge
And held me weeping to his heart
He loved me, he said, though I'd promised
To take him and then wanted to go
And I said to him then in trembling words
Don't kill me, I said
I can be Black Shawl or even Black Buffalo Woman
For my names are legion

Oh, Slow Bear, my mother!

How black his eyes are,
How shining the air that entombs him
And cold the sorrow
How I squirmed and feared and grew sick in his embrace
Swallowing my revulsion
Mouth to mouth with him, my tasting his death
Keeping silent
In terror

Strange man of the Lakota
White as birch, bone powder
A star
How often he walks into lands
Beyond death where no one follows

Oh, Slow Bear, my mother
He knows, like a risen man
The depths of fog and sea and pasture
With his tongue, he was able
To probe my heart
And taste
Its shadows

And find me, Mother,
And know my name

Spilling seed he shuddered
Turned onto his back and wept
Like a child in the dark for a long time
In sorrow
And cried out for his woman, his Black Buffalo Woman
But I am she I said, my names are legion
I love you, he said, but no
Then shrugged, as if he were throwing the cloak of his soul
From his shoulders, and said, in a cracked voice
In a voice as weary as a last voice on earth
He would let me go
He would let me go

Oh, Mother, I'm a woman

So we walked from the lodge and into the green forest
Into the bower of birds
And he let me go, saying
Run if you want to
Just like that…and with ice in his eyes pointed to the forest
Where there would be sweet berries
And paths of earth and air worth taking
And the joys of the world

Oh, Mother, I'm weeping

He is not human. There is nothing human about him
Yet, for one moment only, when I turned to look at him
Walking away
Into cedars into shadow
My heart rode his shoulders

It was a sacred occasion

I await your coming

In this haven of sweet marsh hay

From Crazy Horse's Woman

Black Shawl: And There I Wept

In the lodge of Crazy Horse
I laid myself down
And there I wept
At the snowy moon's passing

And there I wept
My black hair shinning
As the hair of a child

And, Mother, I said, I woke and wept
Putting my fingers inside me and turning naked in the lodge,
Half bent over, moaning and turning, feeling Crazy Horse inside
me.

Touching the crown of the head of the new infant Crazy Horse left
Upside down and deep in my body

Then rose in the dark and four winds screaming.
"Crazy Horse, Crazy Horse. Hoye!"

The women of the village were crying in the distance; the men
were shouting.
It was far away. Far away!
Around many bends of the Little Big Horn

But still I heard the multitude of strong shouts
And mocking voices echoing down the river like thunder. I
groaned a few times, naked in Crazy Horse's lodge,

Naked at the entrance where the sun could see me.
I groaned for my warrior and called out for the pony to bear him
swiftly
For the air to shield him.

Crazy Horse! I cried.

And I said, Mother, it's a baby inside me
It's a baby that stirs and breathes
Inside me
And my mother said yes and it belongs to all men now
For all men are Crazy Horse and all men have hurt you
All men, like Crazy Horse, have hurt you and raped you
And told you they loved you
And took you, like Crazy Horse
This is your mother, Slow Bear, who talks to you of murder
Take the knife from behind you
Put it into their hearts

From Crazy Horse's Woman

Black Shawl: Smaller Than A Star

So Crazy Horse
Stopped for a fresh horse
And I was beside him
In buckskin and beads
With the knife behind me
My breasts heaving, in sweat
In the rush of his heart

There is a child inside me, I said,
Smaller than a star
And his birth shall be wondrous

So Crazy Horse moaned
Like an animal. Falling away

But his eyes were shining
And lifting my dress
He put his fingers inside me
His nails red with bleeding
And touched the child's crown
Smaller than a star
His fresh pony, shifting, waiting
The cries of the dying
Sounding in vagaries of wind
From Grassy Grass and Rosebud Creek
To the Little Big Horn

It will be a good birth, I said
His arms tightening around me
The knife still behind me

In revelry, in its cold breath
And spirit of the wolf

In the smell of his blood
And the death riding in him
In the wolf leaping from him

In the night descending in the full light
of day

Oh husband, I cried, the birth will be easy
The child will come to the earth upside down
As if riding a swift horse

Then the great god, Crazy Horse, trembling
Backing away
Let my dress fall to my knees

His fresh pony, shifting, waiting
The cries of the dying
Sounding in vagaries of wind
From Grassy Grass and Rosebud Creek
To the Little Big Horn

Lakota drums sounded
Of Sitting Bull's dream

And the knife held behind me
Shook in my hand

From Crazy Horse's Woman

Black Shawl: Death Immemorial

It was then I understood
That he was death immemorial

Not human, but an emblem beyond time

Exploding into meaning
By the infernal machinery of days and nights

And grinding of the stars

That is why the heavens are so black
To rise up a son

That is why the earth is so drenched with death
To rise up his son

And now a son is rising inside me

The action of death is like the white man's machinery, the eternal clanking
To rise up a sun

It was then I sensed Crazy Horse's son riding inside me

Oh mother I am a woman

So, I held the knife up again
Crazy Horse was sleeping, or I thought it so

His eyes were open, watching in darkness
Not unsympathetic

I cannot advise you on this matter

He said solemnly, his voice quiet
In the darkness

In the absence of his own mother
Who had already risen to the sky in smoke

In the absence of Black Buffalo Woman
For whom he cried, like a child

Then I heard the death in him like a rushing of warriors
To the Little Big Horn. I heard the sound of hoofs
And the voice of the golden horn

Crazy Horse innumerable was pounding from the chest
For he lived in all time as an emblem of death

And there is no event or man or woman on earth
That does not collide with the eternal

So I heard the pounding of his heart in my own brain
Where I lived innumerable as an emblem of birth

As birth storm, as Black Shawl, as Black Buffalo Woman
And a great cry rose from me for I had seen the truth

And before my eyes a thousand snows
Turned into a thousand springs with flowers
The mutable became the immutable

And Crazy Horse walked the earth as a principle
As all of us walk. In collusion with the eternal forms
And meanings of ourselves

So his passing would accomplish nothing

I loved him too. So, I lowered the knife
And cut myself from the back of the tent
And then I was gone

Outside this window
Rain falls to the bay and the bay
Angles to the jetties built
To preserve the sand
And I remember vaguely
Holding my infant son, somewhere
Maybe by the crosses of this window
Or on the beach or perhaps
Beside the railing of one
Of the stilted wooden decks with benches
Cantilevered over a bluff
To be close to the sea.
The place is not important.
What is, was that I held him
As a father, and he rode
The rant of space
Encapsulated by my arms--
No thought that
There would ever be an end to me
That stars may wash away
Or the heavens fall apart
Until his small body
Slipped though my arms, almost.
His eyes opened,
Looking up.
I whispered something I don't remember what.
Too late, I think.
He knew, or guessed my death
Or so I thought

Occohannock Road

It is easy to love the smell of horses
and urine-soaked hay

With the Chesapeake behind it...dung in the stables
Stars in the pasture... leather

and spring rain

Your whole body slips
into the confluence
Of hoof and sail, withers tremble
Easy Clifford plods paths of sojas

and boysenberry

Trail dust settles softly
on the waters of the brain

Empire

At nightfall
west from Crisfield through
Tangier Sound
The orange boat moves on
to the isle of Deal

Nets of snow tumble to the water dark

In the waning sun
south of the Choptank the fast land
disappears. Hummocks of pine and oak
give way to icy tumps

Captains
of bateaus and dinky skiffs
begin their prayers
Reaching the shallows
the orange boat feels its way
down trenches of tidal gut
through thoroughfare, drain
and little swash of sucking marsh

From over a shoulder, the pale moon comes
thin as a lure and shining
There, in widgeon grass and wild, wild celery,
silage from the marshlands flow,
the spiky corn grass
ripples in windrows, or lies
in cowlicks damp and sticky

My orange boat parts the Spartan flora, the sea lettuce
the eelgrass
The mud banks quake and hold its bow
And caught like fish for a moment only
we are lost in the dark netting

that circles the globe
and rules the world
There you are, the dredge boat captain laughs
And so we are

Thinking of the cypress
 in the black water of the Pocomoke
 of the great depth at which we find
   images of ghosts and things now gone

of the osprey, white
 the teal
 mallard
 railbird
 loon and canvasback

Thinking of the islands vanished
 into the Chesapeake
of Holland Island
 whose schoolhouse, church and houses
 broke off in chunks and drowned
Thinking of the original floating theater
 Showboat, closed down
 and drifting
Thinking of the dark haul of all
 the wide-eyed once familiar faces
 now sinking or sunken
Thinking of all the souls now settling
 like ballast
   into the Chesapeake
into the empire of the whistling swan

Parramore Island
(for Tom Horton)

Under a shoal of stars,
the Atlantic surf
murmurs like ghosts
on the sandy
coasts of the barrier islands

east of Wachapreague and Quinby.

Parramore Island sails the troubled
eons of nautical history like a ghostly schooner
of the mind, appearing, disappearing

...at the edge of the world, Tom Horton says.

      Edges abound, everywhere
with life, with fecund migrations of fish and fowl.

One finds the deep-down
natural scurrying of briar and shell at the edges
of seasons,

at junctures of forest and field
where startles the owl and the white-tailed deer,

in the deep periwinkled

and oystered mud where the salt marsh
and sea converge, in the exhalations
of the booming deep-sea drum.

What fish may swim on the edge of sleep
and wakefulness?

My son, my son,

Where have you gone in the wide world?

The Atlantic surf murmurs
of hole and bar and reef,
as Tom Horton says, in a subsonic voice heard by gulls
on the Barbary Coast

of Africa.

Edges live everywhere
in the latticework of the mind.

The gulls hear each murmur
of the moon-drenched surf
of every salt creek and curve
of Parramore Island as shadowed vibrations
in bone and skull.

Age-old migratory paths
rush from Africa to the Chesapeake Bay,

as Tom Horton says.

It's an awful world to wander in
when you are young and have lost your bearings.

In the hush of ambient
twilight at Parramore
amber foxes detach themselves from the dunes' shadows,

finding in their earthy haunt
the secret edge of poetry.

*Based on an essay by Tom Horton

Pure Winter Comes

Pure winter comes and the bitter cold puts the sooks to sleep
Across the watery avenue swim the herring, shad, and menhaden
the potting's slow and the turbaned black women
leave the shedding
float to pick soft crab by furnace light
beyond the bitter groans of the skipjack's hull
and dreams of cull, dredge and tong

Out on the bay, a schooner having left Baltimore harbor
tugs along its yawl, like a mother her child.
Even sea birds blowing south, over Old Point Comfort
glide thoughtfully, as if listening...

The Maryanne sails wing and wing, catching fore and aft
the strong stern winds that make for a heavy,
wet, and rolling ride

As the crabs forecast - turning to sun and moon
bellies white as snow
the Christmas cold, moving over the water
will be late and easy

Windlass Chantey

"Men who had seen her drank deep and were silent," say the
Clancy Brothers, "Women were talking wherever she went."

1

(Wheeeeeeeeeee)

Out of the spray
of the Chesapeake
comes running the schooner
Enchantress B.
fore-gaff sails set
topsails aloft
past Cape Henry Light
and dreaming, spotless
her horseshoe
holding luck

at the Samson post
her decks fresh
holy-stoned
cream white
she hauls
to starboard
rounds into the wind
to shoot the narrows
past Old Point Comfort
and boom for harbor
And, oh, how immaculate
her wings
her fittings, planking, spars, and shrouds
knights heads and haws

Now, windlass tight
she pays off again

to the whistles of soldiers
at the earthen works, otherwise
dumb, in wonder
Then all the crew leaps
from rigging and mast
the way is checked
by head sails, thrown suddenly back
and from the chain lockers
the cable shudders out
for its first thirsty drop since
the China Sea.
Even the gulls are standing by
pumps are shining
by the galley stack
yards are braced, parallel
the tasseled crew leaps into the rigging
to furl
the luffed skysails
a warp is hurled
and all hands together on the capstan bars
crank her to port with a chantey of a deep
sea voyage

(Wheeeeeee)

2

O the work is hard and the wages low
Leave her, Johnny, leave her
The work is hard and the wages low
O it's time for us to leave her

O I thought I heard the old man say
Leave her, Johnny, leave her
You can go ashore to collect your pay
And it's time for us to leave her

3

On the first day
in the low green and sacred hush of leaves
the light was keeping its own company

And on the second day
did I imagine you here breaking the
water's dark
or was it light that was moving from
tree to tree?

And then, long ago, on the third
day, the river was flowing
and the white birds flying were
paths of autumn

and you were my children on the
fourth and fifth day

All hands and faces and knees of
them like light releasing
through the sixth day to tender
callings

Out past the grave on the final day

As if to old men who adore you so
that heaven seems less dear than
light they know

Mate Dreams of the Canaries while Dying in James Town

We were...

Six weeks from England's shore
In irons. Before we died and died
Some more, at last blew in the bright
Canaries. Of them, we dreamed

Calthrop's bones lie two feet
Beneath my head, his shattered leg
Having ruptured a major artery
We can't sleep but nightly pray

After all is known, as Newport said
We should have stayed in the islands
But Smith and Calthrop would not be led
And talked alone in the evening shade
Before we died and died some more
We could have whaled the Biscay shore
A musket shot and bone remain within
The bone. We had women by the score

Rum ran freely through our veins.
The purple isles, the dyes of orchilla.
Archipelago of wine and banana fruit.
Smith is chained for mutiny. Calthrop

Watched, was later shot in an old
World lately new; then buried lost
As camp compost, with frost his shroud.
Salt hath taken the coffin wood

What can't be helped should be
Forgot. It's all right, for thy shilling, mate
Jesus stood where thou art now
And kissed his bony pate

So what's to think of Paradises left
Behind, the unwilling Christs whose
Bloody footsteps guide men's fate
Here's what we saith: we've

Failed in wit, failed by sword
Failed by courage, failed by word
Failed in effort, failed intent
Failed in dying, and are failing yet

More known to wilderness than hearth
And home, we've lost to pain and pawn
All that once we might have claimed
For names that do but linger on

Odysseus

In a winged conviction
Black rictus of wind and spiraling eye
The curled sail is torn from its clew
I know the manhood of this weather
The spinning mirrors

So much for Ithaca, New York
The bloom is off the myths
Of rose. The fall is due. I cannot swim
I am sixty-six in October
Who shall string my bow?

In my tired room, I think
To drudge from bed to computer screen
My kidneys bleed and the gods play drums
The shells! The mud! My paper gulls!
In acid rain slumps the albatross

I have dined on Penelope
Telemachus, son! Look toward home!
Spied through the fat end of an extended glass
The dolphin devolves beyond the carnal stone
Beginning or ending, the music's done

I preach in college, having
Won my fame in the bowels of a horse
What Stygian suds floods this shingle
Where I've landed? Achilles warned me
Hector's curses hang like laundry

Ajax's suicide is oddly duh rigueur
Pound's old bitch, gone at the tooth
Is mad with grinning. Epically speaking
My children mock me moan for moan
I take a small step, as if to cross my room

Circe plays to ears of wax
In the shadows, the moon finds me
Uninteresting, naked and alone,
Prufrockian. No proof of disc nor dat
A pale expanse of ghastly illumined skin

Fly Hades' bireme, Myrmidon
Of my soul, to storm the citadel of poetry
My feet, at least, are on the floor.
I'm standing. The stars descend, dropping
As snow on an isthmus mooring

Nobody remembers Homer's children
I tell myself. I'm a horrible father,
Vilified, no less, by those I haven't left
What longship bears an old man's shields--
Blindness? Frailty? Love of sleeping?

Drifts of meaning? What nexus?
Meaning drifts, as in-before my eyes
Even as a child, I sensed overwhelming
Complexity, pantoums…was more or less
Certain God didn't know everything…

Thought Moses a fool after the bloody
Foreskin brawl and rescue by Zappora.
Achtung, Jehovah! So grew I, No One, a blister
A boil, a stake in the eye, filled with loose taunts
In a shaky boat on the eventide

The bottoms of my pajamas rolled
Trickster, I, begin a shuffle across my room
Where poetry thrives in counterfeit
Verse that must be completed, then rehearsed,
Then spoken aloud before the mast

My people died in storms at sea

Of rocks, stones, smoke, fits, and slaughter
But I'll sail, praise Woe, lachrymose, but better fed
On honey dew, to scops' fjord
On ashen knarr by way of prelude to my hollow

Not Valhalla! Alas, Ted Hughes
If crow could see me now, taking a pass
On the mystic synergy of the universe
My hair not black, nor set in root by blood
But languid, sprawled, about my head

In crystalline cacophony. Don't I hate
This foolish sundog, now I cry!
Thumbing concave back waves like a jinni
In the morning I break up, mend all the afternoon
Aw, these ugly boomers, hurdling by

Coins from my eyes will pay the boatman
On the other side. My computer weeps
At news I'm coming. I'll stop at nothing
Mix my metaphors, jamb my ends
Leap caesuras   pause   amend

Savant, at sea, at last, neglecting daughters
I'll cross this water, put pen to paper
Metaphorically, in other words
Employ said computer to end all wars
Crying out, I am Odysseus

Poet of all men finned and born
To swim in thrall ad infinitum
And never make it home in a timely fashion
Here, then, is my apologia. I've been old
For more than twenty centuries

I'm rotten wood, crumbled stone, and
Forgotten ash, blown to must and gory
Verse by verse, in obtuse tomes of ancient poetry

All singing's holy. Dreams of the rood
Engorge the channels of my blood

It's no fault of mind that I'm not dead
Blame the furies. Overrated jerks
Who've lost real interest in their work
Whither have the sisters gone?
All night long blows Cape Sable's horn

I wonder why. I wonder why

O Osprey, injured, nursing wounds
  in the morning vapor
of leafy twigs
  above the trembling water

Lazarus too must have known
  some wintry weather
When he rose cold in the wild wet
  straw
    of Bethany

And found its noisy hosannas
  come back for him
And budding like Psalms to lift the
  pall
    of coming snow

Think how he, knowing better, must
  have turned
    from every shadow, and how
    cold it was
in spite of all that gabble
How he must have known warmth as
  illusory

Even as he followed in stinking
  flesh
  the flaring sun
To Jerusalem and then to the frigid
  dark
    of the Mediterranean and its
      vanished coral

Bird, oh how the sky betrays us
With its every shining flower

   and blushing star
It's always so

Beneath the rose the blackness gathers
   and the cats are biting
And Lazarus himself betrays us,
   dear,
Fluttering up ghosts of second chances

Vija's War

Part One: On the Paved Road to Riga

At my grandparents' house
On the paved road to Riga

In the wind of Saulkrasti by the Baltic Sea

Flowers blew in their beds
By the lilac hedge and the linden trees

And I sang my girlish way
To the age of eleven

From garden to store
From post office to meadow
With apples and plums
Chin high in dahlias
And blue with berries

Half moons of cherries

Train stations and forests and gooseberry bushes
An orchard, sweet tea, verandas of mosses

Roses grew in their beds in front of our bedroom window on the
backside of the house and more flowers sprang up all the way
around to the well. There was a vegetable garden...

...rich, ripe strawberries and lilies of the valley

Each morning a shivery sun blushed to be born
Each morning a shivery sun blushed to be born

At my grandparents' house

On the paved road to Riga
In the wind of Saulkrasti by the Baltic Sea

Part Two: Winter

An oven for bread and burners for cooking
A table in the kitchen and a basin for bathing

Grandmother baked the black rye bread for us and for the store to
sell

The aroma of "pirags" wafted from every holiday window
And on top of the stove, my clothes lay drying
Winter apples, hoarfrost, apple dumplings, sun glow

We filled buckets at the well so there would be water the next
morning. The well worked by leverage, like a seesaw. How we
groaned and strained to lift the icy water up

Seesaw, Seesaw
On the paved road to Riga
In the wind of Saulkrasti by the Baltic Sea

Mother and Livija Korps and Miss Licia were elementary school
teachers
Mimitante had a car, I loved Uncle John
I remember my father's face less
Than I remember him coming home late
And fumbling at the door… with his keys

He had left with a barmaid by the time I was four

Seesaw, seesaw
I would sing on the porch, riding Grandfather's ankle
Seesaw, seesaw
I would ride, from the air to the floor

The snow in my hair ... Moonshine

Seesaw, seesaw
I would sing

Closed shutters... packed ice breaking in darkness, in shadow...
blue- green caves
Grandmother's snoring. Seals barking, seals of the mind... Nothing
like traveling through time.... Covered with snow, the great sand
dunes were perfect for sledding.

Hush Vija, hush. There's snow in the pines

Part Three: Sun and Shadow

Summertime was lovely.

Cousin Biruta always came to stay. She was my playmate then

Summer was the time to climb the linden trees, sit on the top
branches, on top of the world, and dream of stories about
princesses and princes on white galloping horses

I ran through the meadow, between the fruiting trees, the warm
summer winds flying through my hair

Doing cartwheels in the meadow

Soft grass
The dirt roads in Saulkrasti were of soft white sand
The delight of cool dew, raspberries, gooseberries, currents,
cherries, plums, apples

Days got shorter, the dusk settled in. Shutter time came
The shadows of the trees got longer, shadows casting shadows. It
was always my job to run around the house, to close all the shutters

A shadow of crawlspace crawled under the veranda. I sneaked by
to close all the shutters, to close all the shutters of the bedroom
windows, to close all the shutters of the living room windows

Who knows what shadows might live along the paved road the
Riga…the garden and Linden trees…the forests of Saulkrasti and
waves of the Baltic Sea?

I would race around the corners of my Grandmother's house
Closing all the shutters in the forests of Saulkrasti by the Baltic Sea

Part Four: If a Knock Ever Came

 Dark whispers fell from the linden trees to shadowy places and
slipped in between the slats in the shutters

*It was a forest time of bears. We children huddled together in bed,
listening to grown folks' talk. The Bolshevik army crashed across
the Eastern border. At our country school, the Russian language
was added, and some of us wore new navy blue pleated skirts,
white blouses and red neckerchiefs!*

*There were whispers of partisans hiding in the woods by the paved
road to Riga…of trains to Siberia…smoke curling from engines
over the Baltic Sea.*

Someone blabbered something to the policeman's daughter

*More rumblings of trains, cattle cars of old people and babies. The
kitchen grew hot making bread for my uncles in the woods. Biruta
and I would hide under the lilac bushes every time a Russian army
truck would go by on the paved highway*

Oh, my Latvia

There were whispers of grandparents Zoka, of Bikernieki of Riga,
near the Bikernieki forest. The Bikernieki forest was the cemetery
of Jews and resisting Latvians, they whispered...

If ever a knock ever came
If ever a knock ever came we would run away at once and hide in
the forest
Of Bikernieki

One night the knock came and our neighbors ended up in
unmarked graves
Russian trucks traveled east, full of ripe soldiers

There were whispers of the dead, the rattling off of cattle cars for
slave labor camps in Siberia

One night in our wandering...in the leaves of moonlight falling
from trees...in the forest
Of Bikernieki

We found a grove of sleeping children, my Biruta and me

Hush Biruta, don't tell
Don't tell, Vija

Their faces alabaster, like moons, their arms limp, like tendrils

In the whispers of Saulkrasti by the Baltic Sea

Part Five: Piparkukas

Christmas, same as Easter and Vasaras Svetki (the Day of
Ascension)
Lasted three days

We had guests from Riga

Swastikas on the planes, Oh look Biruta! They are bombing the railroads
And the Russians are leaving
Blasts trembled the windows

"Deutchland, Deutchland, uber Alles" we sang in the school yard,
"Kamer biksem notrukst snalles"

"Until suspenders break on your pants"

Mother and grandmother were baking from cock's crow. Early in the morning

black rye bread, white bread, pirags, and biezpienkuka (cottage cheese cake)
filled the big oven

Coffee breads wafted through the house at Saulkrasti by the Baltic Sea

At night, while we slept

The drifts grew deep
Blown snow reached the top of a fence

In the winds of Saulkrasti by the Baltic Sea

It was crystalline, it was shining
Vegetables bulged the cellar. We were swollen with winter
Soft wool from Riga, underclothing, heavy shirts and pants

Knit stockings and leggings and the temperature at zero

Grandfather went off to the Bikernieki forest and came back with a tree
Then came the decorations:

Ornaments of straw. Frosted piparkukas strung on the tree. Hard apples, sipolini, the size of small onions, Christmas candy wrapped in colorful fringed papers, brinumsvecites (sparklers), candles for the Lord and white angel hair

Dear Lord, please save those little children sleeping

Biruta, say your prayers.

There were whispers of Riga heard through closed doors
Coughs and silences, the footsteps of my mother

There were partisans coming out of the woods and joining the Germans to chase the Russians from Latvia
Young men joining the German army, Latvian divisions to fight for our country
There were tears and memorials for those murdered and deported
Prisons were thrown open so everyone could see…

Not a word of the children

"Eight," I remember, said Biruta

"No," I said, "There were ten."

Part Six: Swallowed by Waves

1943. The little ghosts were frightening chickens in the yard

Goodbye Childhood, goodbye Biruta
It was a dark time in Latvia…restrictions on everything

SS officers waddled on the shores of the Baltic Sea

We knitted our sweaters and made shoes of wood and old tires
with cloth strapping, like sandals, and mended and mended old
rags of clothing
Ate black bread and cottage cheese, yogurt and porridge
Worried our priests, their bodies like feathers

Down the paved road from Riga, trucks brought the wounded
German and Latvian soldiers, all sticks and bones and crying in
blood and their wrappings

No hands or no eyes or no arm or no legs or no leg or no feet
Nightmares of Cossacks, Russian guns, Russian snows

Frostbitten cheeks and noses, bitten ears and faces
The shifting of bulk, the groaning of cots
The terrible word, *Leningrad,* uttered over and over

We gathered plants by the roadside and beat them into medicines

Still, the soldiers lay turning
Crying out for their dead

Crying out for their mothers and sleeping in our kitchen
Or sleeping in the dendrite in torchlight or on the front porch
tucked into blankets with hot bricks tucked into their bellies
Or sleeping in the kerosene heated tents on the edge of the
Bikernieki forest

Of passing us by, or passing us by after stopping for a moment
And then moving on toward the Baltic Sea
To be swallowed by the waves…it was whispered

Oh my Latvia

I was taught to slaughter chickens by wringing their necks
I was taught to be silent when the SS led the cattle away

And the little ghosts fluttered in anger in the Bikernieki forest

Along the paved road the Riga…in the forests of Saulkrasti
To the crashing of waves in the Baltic Sea

Part Seven: Goodbye, Goodbye

In October we celebrated a day of remembrance of the deceased,
In the old part of the cemetery shaded by trees

In the afternoon, late, it got dark in Latvia with lighted candles and
the singing of hymns. I would sing my heart out

To pass the time

I would go to the railroad station to meet the trains
The woods across the road from the cemetery itself would sob in
its sleep
And I would run…as fast as I could
to the open road by the railroad crossing
Where the dead children stood, sometimes
On the paved road to Riga…by the Bikernieke wood
In the Saulkrasti Forest by the Baltic Sea

We went to Piekusis farm to help cousin Lilija and her husband

Janis had had a stroke from living in fear
and was confined to a chair. Biruta was visiting

Piekusis had a son, Imantso. Two young women helped with the
work.
Besides cutting hay, tending cows, feeding pigs in the pen and
chasing them from the pen to the barn, we gathered linden
blossoms from the blooming trees
and dried them for tea

Trains stopped at the railroad station for half an hour or so.
Grandmother and I would go down with water buckets and
sandwiches for the wounded.

Some would be dying in their seats, some sitting up and asking for
water and cigarettes, some lying in their blood and moaning…they
were so many
We and other women that used to come went quickly…from
soldier to soldier….
No time to change soaked bandages.
We would pray for each one, later…when the train disappeared
around the bend
Throughout the summer we heard a distant rumbling
Like thunder…on clear sunny days
It was time to move West…to relatives in Riga, down the paved
road

In the rumbling storm of tanks and artillery
Mother packed our suitcases and bought tickets on the train…to
stay with uncle Kola and aunt Hermine. Aunt Lilija, Irma and
Biruta had already left for Kuldiga, Western Latvia, where Lilija's
deceased husband had relatives.

Grandmother and Grandpa would not leave the forests of
Saulkrasti

Goodbye Vija
Forever, Vija

The soldiers will fight, they will regain ground, my father said.

We arrived in Riga… in the ruins of Riga
Where the markets were empty and the stores were in ash
Those who had their own gardens had some vegetables to eat

A friend of uncle Kola and aunt Hermine invited us all for supper:
"Komm morgen wieder" (Come again tomorrow)

"Horse's meat!" said my mother

It tasted so sweet

Everyone was fleeing,
west to Kurzeme and in boats to Germany
Aunt Hermine was expecting. Ojars was a year-old, uncle Kola's
father lived in Valdemarpils in the northwestern part of Kurzeme,
so we fled to Valdemarpils while the trains were still running

Where was Mimitante? Uncle Alfred's wife? Aunt Hermine?
Guntis stayed behind

Uncle Ernest disappeared, digging trenches for the army.
Uncles Kola and Alfred, I believe, escaped with their wives and
small children.

I do not remember how long we stayed in Valdemarpils.
I think it was towards the end of summer that we left Saulkrasti.
I am not quite sure when we left Riga and arrived in Valdemarpils.
I do know that we were there in November.
Riga fell to the Russians October, 1944.

In my dreams the ten dead children were standing together on the
paved road to Riga
Having left their places of sleeping, their grove of green trees
In the Bikernieke Wood

Goodbye Vija, Goodbye Biruta

I remember a Priest chanting in an unknown language.
In the snows of Saulkrasti by the Baltic Sea

Song of the Musicians

First Musician

For Jubal, father of flute and lyre
I lift my double pipe, cymbal, and tambourines
To play the hymns of Psalms for Kings

Second Musician

For Solomon, David, and the Lord
I play for victories of the soul and sword
With trumpet, castanets and strings

Third Musician

And how my reed can prophesize
With oaten stop a vanished reign
Or shake wild palms where rattles swing

Fourth Musician

And oh, the whirlwind of the heart
I celebrate with word and note
Both sun and shade. I play my part

All Musicians

These things I remember
    As I pour out my soul
How I went with the throng
    And led them in procession to the house of God,
With glad shouts and songs of thanksgiving,
    A multitude keeping festival.

Fightin' Man

Old Jefferson's
Eyes blared, you know
Wide open
You could see the devil
Tugging
Out his soul

Saw a baby brought up
Went to reaching
Into the box
Crying out
To save its papa

Backed me off from
Funeraling anymore

Big difference then
People came
In the plain weave
To set with the body
Help dig the mud
Hammer the wood

No one was paid nothing
Wanted nothing

Men and women singing
Washing the body
Making clothes for burying
On warps from Kentuck

No charge for the preacher

Church bells tolled once
For every year old

Never personally knew
No body leaving
Where he was put

The dead know nothing
There's nothing they know

Some was buried in shrouds
Time ago, but now
They're most sure
To lay you out in black clothes
Less you're a woman
And to ask before
For some wildflowers
Of pink, or rose

Men was dressed in suits
Slit down the back

Children in white
Likely to get up

At night

The only ground we've conquered
Is right outside our doors

Somebody brought candles

Heard the stiff body
Crack

Rubbed color to the cheeks

On the lids
Laid silver
To get the eyes closed

Jefferson's old wife
Saw his birthmark

First time

When he was laid out

Cold

Evocation

In the morning mist of the Choptank
     down the scudding sea
To the Chesapeake and its tunneling waves
To the slam dance of sea and stars
      in the stick of board and tar
      the groan of hawser
      yowl of jib and spar
      in the long bay wind
I sail in my orange boat and the day begins
      on the Nanticoke
      the Wicomico
      the Pocomoke
And in St. Mary's City

"Because of their steady diet of seafood," says Dr.Foster of
Gloucester, "the women hereabouts are the most beautiful in the
world."

      The whoosh of keel
      the push of sail
I reach into the morning wind and find
  the Age of Steam
When the big freeze came
      and left the Patuxent sheeted
      in fields of ice
and off the Virginia capes all the dredges
      framed
by necklaces of white

I remember I remember
the gusts of freezing rain
the motionless tributaries
     the swollen James
the ice breaker Annapolis
      chuffing in its track

I remember the big ships-
Kate Darlington
and City of Norfolk-
trapped by the ice's mass
        Smokey Joe steaming out
        in flakes of snow big as a hand
        trailing smoke from his stack

"Ol' Cap'n Perry of the Love Point Ferry"
        to the rescue
        from the chill of Love Point
        to the balladeers of Baltimore
"Ol' Perry of the Love Point Ferry"

I remember I remember
        Point Lookout and Point Look-in
        Point-No-Point and Point Again ,
and the last Dutch windmill on the edge of the
        Honga River
the last ferries-Princess Anne,
        Pocohontas, Del-Mar-Va-now
dead and plying still
        a misty trade from Kiptopeake
        to Norfolk

the various sentinel lights:
        Thimble Shoal, Wolf Trap
        and huddled ghosts
        the Drum Point light and the light at
            Thomas Point
both slung, low on stilts, like prehistoric spiders
and the bobbing, rocket lights
        at Hooper's Island and Sandy Point
        that above the brooding water
        rise in cylinders, lit like candles

and I remember all the names of the mollusk towns

      still on the wind
 Oyster, Virginia
 Oystertown and Shelltown
 and Bivalve, Maryland
and the names of towns of the Eastern Shore
 that come on moccasins:
 Nassawadox, Chincoteague, Assateague,
    Machipongo,
 Onancock and Assawoman

I remember I remember
the tales of plunder, of piracy
     in its golden age
and the oyster wars, of geese that
     flew in squadrons, wave on wave
till the sky turned black
and filled with flapping

   "If you couldn't of took a hunnert a day back then
      at glut time," says the waterman, rain-slicked
   in yellow. "it was black gum against thunder."

I remember I remember
     shades of sink boxes
the shadows of gunmen standing in sink
     boxes, now outlawed
     murdering geese and ducks
with their swivel guns, their long toms
     now outlawed

the shrug of wave
the yaw of dream
The tidal flat in thin light
disturbs its reeds

 I tack into the morning wind

and find the age of wings

The sun rises, blushing
        Somewhere blood is flowing
in Africa, in Mozambique, in Peru
But here, the night has peeled away and left
a yellow fruit

 All is musical, quiet
Whispers flutter like empty sleeves
Not even cannon boom over the bay
        to frighten the children

How quickly in my orange boat it becomes
        yesterday
 in Canton Hallow
 or Baltimore,
        where even before trucks
  bellowed
the long dock trembled,

        crowded with bateau's selling potatoes-
 all summer long:
 tomato boats
    and wagons pulling melons
 as the black oyster hucksters
        on Pratt Street cried

Zawneeeeeeeeeeeeeeeeeeeeee.

"In those days," says Mencken, "the days chased
        one another like kittens chasing their tails."

Now the ducks are all wooden
        hanging from the rafters of cottages
        swimming on sills behind glass
        perching on tables, peering

96

through pupils pf paint
How they laugh in their heart-pine hearts
        at the whittlers spitting
        and gossiping on porches
        in galluses, galoshes, and caps
                --rocking in twilight
        their sharp knives imaging
fancy ducks for their laps

There is shadow of wind moving on the water—
        beneath the surface the moon
        like a fish, swimming
        at the bottoms of moments
falling on the Chesapeake
        falling on Tangier
 a light morning rain brings its handfuls
    of soft currents
 to the heron (old Fisheyes) listening
            on one foot
                    to the mounting tide

The Piano

The new dead are sitting on their tombstones
      backs to the wind
It appears they are feasting
I have no love but the love of my own rushing heart
How may I deceive you?
Now and then one calls out of the other
      Oh, love...now come to me
      In the darkness, oh

The old dead less hopefully sing
      at mana tide when the day is airish
      and shadows all the go. So it's
Kitty bar the door
      if some sea sider blue hen's chick
      arises a salty voice
      or dim wit mananose of muddy creek
      should have the hide to sob.
The old dead sing boiled-owl tough in shadders
      in the moon's back houses
      stopped up by wind
I have heard them singing to themselves
      at the bottoms
      of wells   in tater corn   two dogs sick
knocked seven ways from Sunday

They have sung in my grandmother's house
  in Melfa
      at my Aunt Kate's house
      in my family's sojas
      in stables
      in the memory of swimming ponies
      in the colors of race horses

They have sung like the wind   neither one
      given rein to slack sheet

                nor tack
Sung in squalls   in Nor'easters   Sung
        taken short   sure as gun's iron
I have heard them singing at Keller Fair
        grounds
            taut as ticks
        spitting fire into spiders
        skinning lice for tiler
In black and white photographs of my uncles in
        livery
        in silks and sulkies
        hung with garlands of flowers
And now the wind blows into my stoved-up heart
        the names
        of the horses
        Wee Willie
        Beatrice Hanover
        Brother Clarence, who never won a race
And my Aunt Antonette
        her bit and bridle
My Uncle Ben, long dead, terrifying on the porch
        his cigar
        black and evil
And my cancer ridden Uncle Len
        on the stone road to death
Throwing a radio through a window
And old George in a ditch
        a car rolling onto him
And Mucken in his few
        dead of a burst aorta

So, at last I am sung into a framework of black and
    white
        of a tinkling piano in an old farmhouse
        of flash and penumbra of my
            Grandpa's children
        their children and their children's children

And my own dead child somewhere in the universe
    dead of some agency, of some future time
      and hand
    and shadow of the rock, dead and dying in
      the watery dark
    drifting as a ghost through the universe
      my own child
         riding the saddle of space
         to Jupiter or Mars
         dying, giving birth

I have come to the black stable of the Cartesian
    clock

Billy the Kid

At first
One is embarrassed, of course
To appear naked at the follies
Then, one adjusts, like an Ute to his pyre
Something dies something's burnt off
I have learned the cowboy Billy the
    Kid
Danced like an angel
In Abilene with death in his arms
Like a giggling girl, flirting with
    Everyone
And dark

One should, said Billy
Beware of hospitals when plague's at
    The window
Scratching like a whore and the
    Stars
Coming out genuflect at the foot of
    The desert
For both these things are portents
    Of nakedness
The wild wet cactus stripped of its
    Whiskers
Grows savage and dead and about its
    Stiff column
The turtle spins and the musical
    Worms
Are not without brass
To begin an old song

Good for them

Last night the nightingale
    Looking for a mate

Swallowed a sliver of the moon
And still the women dance
The beautiful naked women
Dancing in Rome   in Orlando
And Billy and I sure enough dance
    With them
In the several eyes of the mind
Each of us saying
This is my own, my eternal naked
    self
I give you naked my own death and
    Resurrection
And trigger finger of redemption
To the beat of a drum

Silver Beach

Flights of geese
Ply
The shaken avenues
Of wind
Like the filigree
Of a breaking wave

This is my own
My deep blue country

In the morning chill
And blush of sun
The mewing
Gulls
Rise in waves
Of steepled fire

The empowered dust
Stirs
In strings
Of cottages

This is the hour
Of keenest memory

The invisible shore
Shudders
In impossible thunder

There are eggs to think about
The popping of grease
In the iron spider

Still the ghosts

Sit in a fine array
Around the wooden table

Talking of neap tides
And offshore currents

There's no voice here
More important than any other
All are sifting

Into the sunlight
Of the kitchen window
Where Old Kate Bull sings *Abide with Me*
And *O'Donovan Rossa*

People of the Mist

Shelves of light
tier in pink, amber
& jimmy blue

above the Bay Bridge-Tunnel

Through the darkness

falling
Norfolk lights
extend themselves

To the cynosure stars

Eos' fingers of rose
open heaven's gates
& the truck driver stunned

pulls to the rail
at the side of the road

People of the mist
ride the vanished lanes
of Shellfish Bay

A thousand years ago
the Susquahannock
pondered scrimshaw

& fossilized bone
of a thousand years before

Foxes scavenged the watershed
The loblolly swayed

& werowances whispered

of a people like mist
who rode the waves from Kiptopeake
to Elliot's island

& there they stayed
in clouds of ice

on a hammock
of tidal flat shaped
like a horse's shoe

People of watery smoke
& cold intimations

The truck driver hears
their soft canoes

People of the pogonip
Of the Hammock's hoof

Horse Hammock Point

Once, from the wrack lines
I drew the wild sea up
in a snag of drifted wood
from the moon flung chalk
of waves. I heard
that entangled ghost of bitternut
salt riven, hickory
pock and slurp in tongues
of breaking dark's
littoral surge and roll
beyond the reefs
of stalking ice
and Spanish sea
to marshlands of the Virginia
coast, combed by holes
and swept by tide

Then in the sojourn of my mood
I weathered again
the easterlies
of my childhood
the rising flood of shadowed sea
and storms of light
at Horse Hammock Point
I probed again with ear and eye
the hungering crab
in stinging beds of waving grass
and lolling eel,
the shot black ducks'
fluttering, beak-first
demise into silent
pools

and knew then, in my bone
the plunging stars

and saw as if from Mercury
the bleached earth orb,
spinning and dumb
a little spot out there, adrift

in deepening space, like wood
that God could cover with his thumb

Tangier Sound

Now
in the encroaching dark
the dark posts rise
to piers of creosote

The snowy egrets blow to sea
In moonlight now
cricks and guts rive the marsh
They curve in arcs,
crisscross and sinister bend

Landforms pounce, disappear and rise again
Whole towns hunker down

It's good to see your lights at night, says
the Widow Kent

It's a drizzly fog
rolling the breadth of Tangier Sound
Swans bay like ghosts at Horse Hammock Point
The multicolored

Christmas lights go on one by one
Abandoned homes
gone dark
begin their evening
bouts with sea
and wind

The proggers guess
their dark way home
through Cathedral bush and
labyrinths
of bottoms reed and
shrugging wash

Now broadside, Smith Island looms
and now is gone
Now over a shoulder Smith Island comes
contracts and flees
expands

Now in the wind
rides the flowery scent of old Onancock

and the mournful notes
of the Great Blue Heron and black back gull
that float like plums
above the sinking yards of tanagers
and vireos

in a mist that lightly turns to rain

The Lord of crabs sings to me
of just how darkly earthly sin
boards a life and settles in

Zipporah

So my husband, Mosheh,
Took me from the fine tents
Of Jethro, my father, the Priest
Of Midian-
For Mosheh had been an alien
Living in a foreign place
And sought knowledge of his kinsmen
In Egypt, be they quick or dead

And besides, in palms, had counseled
With the Lord like a robber with his chief
To make a fool of Pharaoh

I will harden his heart, said the Lord
He will not let them go

Mosheh trembled, in shadow

Night's cloak, the pelt of an animal
Wrapped all about him
Beneath a snare of stars
Mosheh listened.
A viper, hooded, stiffened in his fingers
His drawn hand
Shone leprous and white, like
Alabaster, and then drawn again
Softened into flesh
Like satin
So, too, to Mosheh's ear
Did a gurgle of waters
Promise blood

Show Pharaoh your wonders, said the Lord
For he will ignore them
I shall harden his heart

He will not let them go

Say to Pharaoh, Israel is my firstborn son.
But you refused to let him go;
Now I will kill your firstborn son.

Mosheh trembled, in shadow

Mosheh, I whispered, in the shadows
Of our bed, in the quiet of ravens
When I had pleased him
Do not trust the Lord
For you are his vessel of water
Turned to blood
And his face is hidden

But still we journeyed to Egypt
Mosheh before me, my heart
Finding shadows in daylight
And at night shadows within shadows
Our child, weeping
Our camel stumbling into dark
The wild palms stirring into storm

Then the Lord
Flung himself upon us, murderous
Rage upon rage, upon Mosheh
Until a flint in my hand
Cut the foreskin of my son,
Smearing Mosheh with blood
And a voice like mine cried
To my husband
Truly you are a bridegroom
Of blood to me...by circumcision
A bridegroom of blood

Then the Lord, God of Mosheh
Let Mosheh alone

And the night grew quiet

And I trembled through my life

Not knowing what I'd done
--beyond flint and blood
By my tongue's convulsion
To save Mosheh with words

Jellies' Song

We are made of water
And know the light
And dark below, and weight of stars
By the ocean's roll
And up or down
By sensor cells that rim
Our souls
We travel light, weightless
In our skins
And hunt in drifts of food
By letting go

And do not dream

Nor do we know
Where our bodies end
And the seas begin
We scarcely flutter, but sting.
We're complexly simple.
Eyeless, earless, bloodless
Baubles of red and white
And royal blue.
We're pretty, friend

And do not dream.

Our trade is drifting
We drift together
Almost invisibly
We die in winter
In the far Antilles
Rebuffed by storms
And do not moan
Or know our names

We replicate ourselves

We swim. And that is key. We swim

Huntin' Creek

At night I dream
of hardening shells
where shallows
drop
to channels
and seagulls, circling, sign
of grass so slick
and smooth
that progmen in their beamy boats
chug the seams
of bottoms' mud
through morning rain

The air is breathless in my head

The sun's a shiver
on the weather shore
and gulls in storms of mewing
grays and whites
follow the dragged iron,
croupier scrapes
that pop live crabs from grass in cards
of fiddler cream
and olive hue
to fill rough hands with peelers soft
as wind, and buckrams in their ancient blue

All night the wind is blowing
All night it cries through my dreams
Like some forsaken sailor man dead
And unredeemed by dying

And unredeemed by dying

You'll catch more crabs when you're out there than when you ain't!

The marshland sings of dreams unending
of waves of grasses black and green
fleshed with flounder, ray
and fattened worm
The sun suspends itself in liquid blue
Smith Island weeps with light
The day is ending

The sea is slaty ca'm, as they say

Now comes a dream within a dream
Out where the buoys
bob tidal urge and doings
waters close over the sea blown
roofs of Tylertown

All night the wind is blowing
All night it cries through my dreams
Like some forsaken poor progger dead
and unredeemed by dying

More arysters down there than we been ketchin'
says old Ben Parks, pulling shut his coat

One-eyed jacks and deuces wild
by the guttering candles.

Man Was Once a Child

Man was once a child
but knew from a puff of air the day's priorities
and from the shadows of his labors
guessed his name

Weatherford, Workman, Cookson
Miller and Hull and Netty and Ty,
Fisher, Farmer, Painter, and Price,
Sassy and May Wine

Heaven help us if it can!

When the wind turned 'round, he pulled
When the wind set fair, he ran

Ain't no such thing as oystermen?
Nor fishermen, nor clammers
Nor proggermen?
Them's watermen, over thar!

Thank you, Mrs. Waterman.

And every one of us is a waterman's woman!
Who's to say we ain't?

Smell of crab on my clothes...every day of my life.

the wind may be found where sailormen
are gathering
it teases the shrouds
chills the upright, licked finger
scuttles the clouds
sends smoke from chimneys
twisting into messages
>drives the sail
>and then feather-light like a breath
>tickles hair on the backs of necks
>makes telltales flutter
>tugs the Cunningham's ring
>and rushing, like water
>eddies, billowing
Then curls from the weather shore
>blowing flags
>leaves
>bells
all morning and beyond

Once the wind spat a diamond into the palm
of my hand
and I let it go
in dread of shadows
endlessly repeating

The wind
This ether
of my imagining
through which the
firelight travels

The wind
ghostly, moving
through the soul

of the universe
as if there is no other
thought
or sea
or rope
or ceaseless star

The wind
white shadow of sailor men
traveling beyond reach of
halyard and spar

Sometimes at the turning on of a lamp
one can catch the flap of a wind
retreating
Catch it for the briefest moment
as if to say
This is what I know. This is where I'm going.

First Fisherman

Into the doors at the front of the house
and the back of the house
and the side of the house
in their unguents and creams
in their pastels, their belts of white,
their ballooning sleeves

First Fisherwoman

in florals, and gaiters and strings
of pearl, in their lotions and waters
they come with their shadows

All

to the doors in the front of the house
and the back of the house
and the side of the house

Second Fisherwoman

they spread out in the parlor
their leather shoes polished
their ears attuned, listening to the clock
where it's ticked for years
in shadows,

First Fisherman

in squalls, in the din of bells
hey you boys get away from the horse
Hot damn! Right on his head

Second Fisherman

Into the back of the house
and the front of the house
and the side of the house
with their shadows behind them

First Fisherman

They come with their shadows
Their shadows behind them
trailing like dogs, or flowers behind them
and the shadows within
who cry like children
First Fisherman

Oh, Mama, I'm here

Second Fisherwoman

Oh, Daddy, I'm lonely

First Fisherman

who cry like the wind of Horse Hammock Point
who cry like lost children
in the windows and blinds
in the front of the house
and the back of the house

All

All with their shadows

First Fisherman

They come with the shadows of themselves

they had thought to
leave behind, somewhere…pieces
of themselves they had thought to leave behind
in cemeteries in Parksley
in Orancock and Belle Haven
or lonely in fields, beside the quiet churches
by the sides of quiet roads
or lonely in fields, beneath stones
in the backyards of Melfa
or plots in Leemont

    Second Fisherwoman

Into the doors at the front of the house
and the back of the house
and the side of the house
they come with their shadows

    First Fisherman

Each finding the other
and speaking of shadows
     Second Fisherman

Each in his remembering
finding shadows of faces
in the faces of the others

    First Fisherwoman

Oh, she's got the Turlington nose

    Second Fisherwoman

Yes, she does, poor child

    Second Fisherwoman:

And look at that boy
The spittin' image of his father

First Fisherman

All the shadows inside them
Crying like the wind at Horse Hammock Point

All

Into the doors at the front of the house
and the back of the house
and the side of the house

First Fisherman

fingering fried chicken and biscuits
of ham on paper plates, heaping on the cold slaw
and pickles and cakes, drinking tea
with their shadows, talking of the weather
settin' down on the porches,
where George Floyd sat and others sat
before him, or settin' down in the parlor
with plates in their laps

All

They come with their shadows

Second Fisherwoman

I'll tell you what
If you're gonna have a tree…as my daddy said
It oughta be a fruit tree…
might as well get something to eat…my
daddy said…

First Fisherwoman

I got enough to eat. A person needs shade from a tree...
that's the main thing.
When the summer comes along...
best thing my mama liked to have overhead was them waxy
magnolia leaves.

Second Fisherman

No, sir. Shade ain't the thing. Best thing about a tree...
makes you remember things...

Second Fisherwoman

Remember Mrs. Belote?

First Fisherwoman

Reckon I do...use to run the store...

Second Fisherwoman

Reckon she did...reckon she did
oh, my.

First Fisherman

In the doors at the front of the house
and the back of the house
and the side of the house
They come with their shadows

All

They come with their shadows... their shadows... shadows...
shadows... shadows

Where Do the Crabs Go?

Where do the crabs go
  leaving their shadows behind them
What presses their return from
  the autumnal reef

In the winter I shall row with a
  stranger beside me
Call him an old hand, ready with the sail
Let the stranger spend his knowledge
  of all things passing
The fiery sun that blushes to be born
The stirrings in the cottages
  and demarcations of the gull
I shall row from the darkness of my
  brain to where charts have no meaning
And my friends of the air cannot see one another

And should you move with me
  sidereally
beyond the shallows
Your petticoats behind you
And the tide at an oar

We may hope to discover no eddying
  of days, or hands, or shoals
Only ourselves-ghosts of light
  and tireless travelers
Some fisherman on the bay will look
  up from his catch and say
  with a blue sook listening
I am a living thing

I breathe and I am dying

But that is not what we'll whisper
        with our voices of shelled things
In our skins of water

Ship's Log, 1841

So this day ends in grief
as the naval books will say
with the weather thick, phosphorous seas
        and the hauling wind prevailing
we took in mizzen sail and jib
        aye, we did, God help her, poor ship
foresail and forestaysail still wavering
        above a trough of breakers
At 2 a.m. we left her
        in breeches buoy, Gentlemen
bumping hard was our lady

And we were all asleep in bed
        when her lashes gave
and wrecked and dead, she set off for Ireland

Easter Sunday, 1980

It is quiet now
Drops of rain begin their silken plunge
To the tender leaves and shoots
      Where darkness if
Hidden in rows, stone by stone

It is quiet now
      in the solar wind

Oh, point of light in the womb of space
      curled in heaven's dark
      like some animal
      waiting to be born or dying
May the black rains rouse the
      metronome and the dead take up
      their lives again

Everything I breathe is prayer

Over the chiming bridge may new worlds pass
To their tears and anvils
      May we hurry home

Oh, once in the dark
      I knew a ghostly shining
Knew it as surely as leaves their
      water as water in the wind has
      its ghostly story

Knew it in my blood as the ram its altar
      and find it now, Ann, in this
      cemetery in Parksley
      where the graves have their light
      every stone its mother

And the words of my love rage round
   Quasar-bright and holy

Rogue's Harbor

Now in a delicious afternoon
of my sailing in slow time
in a father light of shaking sun and reluctant stars
in the time of steeplechase at Fair Hill, Maryland
In the time of railbirds at the
head of the bay and vibrant silks
at Rogue's harbor on the Elk river
the kiteman does his festival stunts, flags wave

From the northern tongue of the North East river
a storm looks southward, dark clouds gathering
Darkness squats on the trees and river houses
lightning parts the water
Shacks along the river that wear their porch roofs
like the bills of hats and year by year slide further
into the water's embrace
close their eyes-
Somewhere within, lamps are burning-
Fallen trees turned white by time, grow gray
at dusk, extend their branches, their twigs like skeletal
fingers

O mother dark
in the dying time
of sundown at Tolchester

the heron waits like a fisherman on a long pier
his head erect
his body in silhouette
an upside down "L" against a rosy sky
his soft flesh and feathers
breakable
(dark posts loom above his head)
He is listening

for jumping fish
to every ripple
to the stolid silence of the unmarked

Indian gravestones of Cecil county
to the wild flower's song
and the ancient battle of Brandywine
He, in darkness, listens
(The shadow of a heron falls across backdrop. Music stops.)
Nobody is more attentive than Harry the Heron.

Old Fisheyes.
Of the earth by one foot only, he listens now to the shadows falling
and the steel drum bands of old St. Croix.

Bounty

An arc of sail
the spilling wind
Off Tangier
the fishermen draw their
purse nets in
and let them out
The sea is breathing
wild with rock, black drum and trout
beneath the Margaret's
dead-rise sharp and hollow hull
The hickory shad, white shad and herring
begin their aching run to spawn
beyond the gill nets
pounds and fykes
to the churning water
of the dark, bright country

The Margaret tosses, as if in prelude to a disturbing night
The fleet waits in softened sun
The strike boat moves out to mark the spot
(with freeboard's creak and raking mast)
in the nursery chill
evening comes
with weir poles, stakes and traps
soft crab, sook, peeler, and peeler buster

The net boats drop their haul seines and
bobbing corks
for croaker, bass, sea trout and perch
for flounder, sharks
for robins of the sea, for toads that puff
for alewife, cheborg, largemouth and blue
for the sea itself and all its finery

What can I give my son
that will be his to keep
though I have given it?

Beyond the darkening
line of shore
the young pitch pines
crouch darkly like shadows

like the shadows of boulders
like strange dwarves rounded, symmetrical

like pygmies with their blowguns
each blowgun filled with rosin
and fine for burning
each branch of gummy timber
igniting, flaming
like a torch

like so many eyes of the Japanese
I hear the naval guns thundering, practicing
I remember Pearl Harbor, the radio
in my grandmother's living room
arched-in memory -
like a cathedral
The massive gray landing craft that pulled
up on the beach in front of my Aunt
Bessie's cottage-for practice

I always hear those booming naval guns
that thunder at night over the bay's broad waters
that thunder in my dreams down the decades of my life
What can I give my son
that shall be his the more
as it moves beyond his keeping?

The darkened pitch pine on shore
send forth from rocks and sand
their stemless cones

Author's Note and Credits

Almost all of the *Selected Poems* have been performed professionally as poem/plays at various times over the last forty years. Many are from produced poem/plays that have been published in playbook form: *Hymn to the Chesapeake* (published by Road Publishers, Have Scripts), *Horse Hammock Point* (Stonehall Publishers), *Music of Leaves* (Stonehall Publishers), *Vija's War* (San Francisco Bay Press), *Chesapeake Celebration* (Playwrights'Premier Theatre of New York), *Threshold to America* (produced and published courtesy of fourteen grants and the Eastern Virginia Brass), and *Crazy Horse's Woman* (London Books). Magazines which have published the author's works include *Ripasso*, *Little Magazine* of New York, *Port Folio*, *BlackWater Review*, *The Ghent Quarterly*, *Poem,* and others.

Arthur's conventional books include *Strokes* (Stonehall Publishers), *Vija's War and other Poems* (San Francisco Bay Press), *Hymn to the Chesapeake* (as a book of poems) (Road Publishers), *Robert Arthur's Eastern Shore* (Scriptworks), and *Black Gum Against Thunder* (Northampton House Press). His *Phaedra* (DHK Publishers) is a play in modern verse. In 1993, *Hymn to the Chesapeake* was produced as a poem/play in Virginia, Maryland, New York, Washington D.C., and St. Petersburg, Russia.

The author built *Windlass Chantey* from an introduction to a song by the Clancey Brothers with Tommy Machem, who built their introduction from an unknown source. *Parramore Island* was built from an article by Tom Horton, who is cited and quoted in the poem. The primary source for the Appalachian poems is the *Foxfire Book* series (Eliot Wigginton and his students). *Appearances* quotes Sam Harris and owes him much. *Vija's War* was based on the life and diary of Vija Martenson. Two poems were inspired by Van Gogh. The author was also influenced by Baltimore pictorialist A. Aubrey Bodine and the writer William Warner. He thanks novelists David Poyer and Lenore Hart for their friendship and assistance, as well as novelist Frances Williams, poet Jeff Hewitt, Carolyn Kreiter-Foronda (Poet Laureate of Virginia), and publisher/playwright Jean Klein.

Poems from this volume recently receiving awards from the Poetry Society of Virginia include "*Sunday Seizure.*" "*Occohannock Road,*" "*Family Reunion,*" "*The Forest,*""*James Town Journey,*" "*Appearances,*" "*Snakes,*" "*Pure Winter Comes,*" and "*Windlass Chantey.*"

About the Author

Arthur's poems focusing on place have been podcast from San Francisco and his poem/plays produced on stage in Virginia, Maryland, Washington D.C., Pennsylvania, New York City, and St. Petersburg, Russia. Robert P. Arthur grew up on the Eastern Shore of Virginia and in Norfolk, Virginia. He has a M.A. from the University of Richmond, where he studied under historian Clifford Dowdey, and a M.F.A. from the University of Arkansas, where he studied under poet Miller Williams and fiction writer William Harrison. He teaches in the Graduate Creative Writing Program at Wilkes University in Pennsylvania. Arthur has written over twenty books of poems and plays, and over a thousand articles on the arts. He lives in Onancock on the Eastern Shore of Virginia with his wife, Gray, and has five children: Nicole, Hannah, Elizabeth, Robert William, and Eudora.

Northampton House Press

Northampton House publishes selected fiction – historical, romance, thrillers, fantasy – and lifestyle and literary nonfiction, memoir, and poetry. Our logo represents the Greek muse Polyhymnia. See our list at www.northampton-house.com, and Like us on Facebook – "Northampton House Press" – for more great reading.

www.ingramcontent.com/pod-product-compliance
Lightning Source LLC
Chambersburg PA
CBHW021405090426
42742CB00009B/1012